BASICS OF PERSONAL FINANCE

1) CREATE A BUDGET

2) WHAT IS DEBT

3) PAY OFF DEBT

4) BEGIN SAVING/INVESTING
   A) Savings
   B) Emergency Funds
   C) Sinking Funds
   D) 401K Traditional vs Roth
   E) IRA Traditional vs Roth
   F) Brokerage Accounts

5) REAL ESTATE
   A) House Hacking
   B) Primary Residence
   C) Investment Property

6) FIND YOUR PURPOSE

7) TESTIMONY

CREATE A MONTHLY BUDGET

The perception of a budget to most people is that it's an obstacle that will prevent them from buying things they want to buy. It restricts them. It will force them to say no, when their friends invite them out for dinner or a good time. It will make them tell their children no, you can't have that toy. On the contrary, a budget does the complete opposite. Imagine knowing that your income for any given month is at a level that is higher than your expenses. Now you can accept that invitation from your friends or allow your child to have that toy, without any guilt. Creating a budget provides you with a feeling of being in control.

The most important function of a budget is tracking your spending. Once you have a handle on your spending and your income, it is imperative that the bottom line of your budget has you spending less than the income you have coming in. There is no possibility of personal financial growth without this. Once you've achieved a handle of your money, you can now tell your money what to do.

To begin evaluating your own personal finance situation, I recommend creating a budget using either a personal budget app, template, or spreadsheet. I've attached a simple spreadsheet as an example. Everyone's budget sheet needs to be customized to their situation.

Once your budget template is complete, list all sources of income throughout the course of the month. This can be income from W2 employment, 1099 or self-employment, side hustle or hobby income, tax refunds, inheritances, gifts, etc. List them all and total them. The sum will be the maximum amount of money entering your household for this particular month.

Next, list all expenses, and I mean ALL of your expenses. Most people don't realize the amount of money they spend on almost any category and will underestimate their expenses. Not knowing your numbers can be detrimental to your overall budget. A simple way to track your spending is to go back through your bank statements for the past three months. Include in this budget each and every expenditure. Create as many categories as you need. This will tell you exactly what you're spending on your rent or mortgage, utilities, groceries, car payments, fuel for vehicles, restaurants, insurances, cell phones, streaming services, the dreaded credit cards, student loans, car loans, personal loans, donations, etc. List all credit cards and loans, showing their minimum monthly payments, not their overall balance. List them all and total them. This is the total amount of money that is leaving your household for this particular month.

Remember, the income total must be equal to or greater than the expense total. There are only two equations to a budget sheet, the income and the expenses. If your income is greater than your expenses, congratulations. You've accomplished the most critical step in personal finance growth without even realizing you've done it. This doesn't mean you're on cruise control. Keep reading, you can always do better. If your expenses are greater than your income, don't panic yet. There are solutions to resolve this.

Increase your income. How can I do this? I already work a full-time job. What else can I do? Ask for a raise. Be honest and ask yourself, do I deserve a raise. If you think you do, write down the reasons why you deserve a raise. If you don't think you deserve one, write down why you think you don't, and work on getting better in these areas.

Work overtime. Somewhere along the line, many people developed the mindset that so long as they work 40 hours a week, then they're doing all they can. Once you get to the end of this book, you'll realize how silly this sounds. There are 168 hours in each and every week. You think you're going to succeed by working less than 25% of the time? How's that working out for you so far? Some people may be able to get away with that, and that's great for them. This logic simply does not work for most Americans.

Develop a work ethic that mom and dad would be proud of. After all, you deserve a better life, don't you?

If overtime simply isn't available to you from your employer, get a second job. This second job might be in the same field as your first job, or something totally different. The possibilities are endless. Your second job doesn't need to be another full-time job. Your second job can be 10, 20 or 30 hours per week. It will depend on what is needed to fix your budget, and how determined you are to begin your journey to success.

Sell things around the house that you no longer have a use for. Almost everyone has things in the back of their closet, in the basement, in the garage, attic or shed, that they've long forgotten that they even have anymore. Take a walk around the house. Look inside some of those old boxes in the basement and see what's in there. When was the last time you used it? Are you better off selling it? You may find that once you sell certain items you no longer have use for, you'll be able to use that money for some utility bills or credit card payments.

Offer your services to friends and neighbors. You may have a useful skill that someone else would be willing to pay for. Mowing lawns, trimming hedges, raking leaves, shoveling snow, painting a fence, securing some deck boards or railing, cleaning gutters, replacing a ceiling fan, power washing, washing a car, changing the oil on a car. There are endless tasks that people are willing to pay a small fee for. I'm willing to bet that you're capable of performing many, if not all of these tasks.

Find a side hustle. The new gig economy is an excellent way to quickly increase your income. The food delivery industry is booming, and easy to get into. You can set your own hours, work as much or as little as you need to.

All these options are not meant to be done forever. The idea is to fix the income side of your budget sheet. The longer you can sustain this, the more it will benefit you in the long term.

Cut your expenses. I'm sure as you went back three months to see where you are spending your money, you've probably discovered things that can easily be cut back. Maybe there's a subscription or two that you haven't used in months. A streaming service or gym membership that are no longer being used.

More likely than not, your grocery or restaurant expenditures were much greater than you anticipated. Oh, where do I start? Instead of stopping at your favorite coffee shop every morning and giving them $5 - $10 every morning, why not make your own coffee at home? For the amount you're spending in one week, you can make your own coffee at home for about three months. Instead of buying lunch every day at the office cafeteria or the local deli for $10 - $15 per day, how about packing your own lunch from home? A sandwich and a couple snacks, or maybe some of last night's leftovers.

Trust me, the only people who will laugh at you are your broke friends. Why are you trying to impress them? Try going to the grocery store once a week. Many people will go several times a week, spending more money than they really need to.

Start with meal planning for the week. Make a list and purchase the items you'll need to make those meals and anything else on the list. The grocery store wants your money much more than you do. They spend millions of dollars setting up their store to entice you to spend more than you anticipated spending. You've worked hard for your money, don't give it away because they want it more than you do. You're on a mission and it's time to get smart.

How do I address restaurants? This is an easy one. If you're at a point in your budget sheet where your expenses are greater than your income, cross restaurants off your "to do" list. You just went to the grocery store, so we know you have food at home. Now you're going to go to a restaurant and spend $50 or more for a meal that you can make at home for $10 - $15? Seriously? There are no judgements made here, we've all made foolish decisions with money and we're on a path to changing all of that.

Maybe turn off a few electrical appliances, unplug a few items, lower the thermostat, and/or caulk your windows. How many times do you leave a room with the intent of not returning any time soon, and leave a TV on or forget to turn off a light? Did you know that unplugging small appliances on the kitchen counter, phone chargers, the tv in the spare bedroom or even the washing machine that gets used once per week, can save you up to $20 per month? Review your cell phone bill and make sure you're not paying for features you don't need to be paying for.

Review your auto insurance policy. If you've had the same insurance company for several years, chances are you're paying too much for your coverage. Insurance companies don't reward you for being a long-time loyal customer. Instead, they typically raise their rates over time, assuming that the typical consumer won't take the time to shop for a better deal. And they're right. Most people won't shop around, but you will.

See a typical monthly budget sheet. Keep in mind, your budget sheet needs to be customized for you and your family. Feel free to create your own budget sheet, modifying the categories to represent your lifestyle.

MONTHLY BUDGET SHEET

INCOME

Job #1	$	-
Job #2	$	-
Job #3	$	-
Side Hustle	$	-
Tax refunds/Stimulus/Bonus	$	-
Gifts / Inheritances	$	-
Additional Income	$	-
TOTAL INCOME	**$**	**-**
Mortgage or Rent	$	-
Electric	$	-
Internet	$	-
Gas or Oil	$	-
Water / Sewer	$	-
Auto Loan	$	-
Auto Insurance	$	-
Auto Fuel	$	-
Auto Maintenance	$	-
Cell Phone	$	-
Groceries	$	-
Restaurants	$	-
Entertainment	$	-
Charity	$	-
Savings / Emergency / Investments	$	-
TOTAL EXPENSES	**$**	**-**
TOTAL CASH FLOW	**$**	**-**

WHAT IS DEBT

Many people have different thoughts revolving around debt. Some will claim that all debt is bad debt. Some will claim that there is a difference between good debt and bad debt. Personally, I feel that some forms of debt are necessary to move forward in your financial journey. At the same time, it's very important to realize how this debt is either inhibiting your growth of wealth or how it is helping your growth of wealth. Here are some examples of varying types of debt.

I just bought an awesome pair of sneakers for $300, that I put on my credit card. I only must make a minimum payment of $15 each month. At an interest rate of 25% and the minimum payment of $15 per month, will result in making payments on this purchase for 27 months and these $300 sneakers that are the coolest things on the market will have cost you $392.17. A $40 pair of sneakers, where you probably could have paid for in cash, would have resulted in making those extra payments towards other loans to get you out of debt or even towards saving and investing. This would be considered bad debt, every time.

    The transmission on my car died and it will cost me too much to repair, so I got a brand-new car for $25,000, but my payment is only $402.23 per month for 7 years. Pretty awesome, huh? After making these minimum payments for 7 years, with a 9% interest rate, you've paid a total of $33,656 for this $25,000 vehicle. Still a good deal? You could have purchased a $5,000 vehicle, either had a much smaller loan with a smaller payment for a shorter period, or maybe even paid cash for it. This would be considered bad debt, almost every time.

    Ok, so now on to the "good debt". You want to purchase a home. With the rising costs of real estate, you just don't have $400,000 to put down on a starter home, so you take out a 30-year mortgage at 5% interest, and your monthly payment (excluding homeowner's insurance and property taxes) would be $2,147. You've purchased your first home, over time you'll gain equity in your property, and more likely than not, your property value will increase over time. However, keep in mind that if you make the minimum payments on this property for 30 years, you will have paid $737,632 for this $400,000 home. Although it's almost always expected that a mortgage will be required to purchase a home, it's almost never required to keep that loan payment for the full term of the loan. Make additional payments as often as you can to limit your overall home expenses.

PAY OFF DEBT

Now that you've created your first monthly budget with a positive cash flow (greater income than expenses), you're now ready to start eliminating those pesky credit card and loan balances. There are two ways of accomplishing this feat.

The SNOWBALL METHOD – This is when you list all your credit cards and loans from the highest remaining balance to the lowest balance. You will take the excess money from each month (making sure you've paid the minimum balances on all loan balances) and pay down the smallest balance. You will continue to do this each month until that debt is totally paid off. The fact that it's the smallest balance means it shouldn't take very long to get paid off. Once this is done, apply the same process to the next lowest balance. You will take the excess money from each month PLUS the money you were paying on the first balance and apply it all to the next lowest balance. The amount you apply to each loan balance as time goes on slowly grows with intensity, simulating a snowball rolling downhill, gradually increasing in size. The same is true for the extra dollar amount you apply to each balance.

The purpose of paying off debt by using the snowball method is strictly behavior. By paying off the smallest balance quickly, you are now gaining the confidence that this is possible. You paid off the first debt, it's time to celebrate. Celebrate quickly and then move on to the next debt. Pay that off and celebrate. Move on again, until all your debts are paid.

An example of the snowball method repayment schedule would be as shown below.

Credit card #1 minimum payment	$150 balance after
Loan to mom & dad	$1,000 balance
Car loan after minimum payment	$5,000 balance
Student loan after minimum payment	$19,500 balance

After all minimum payments have been made, any extra money will be applied to credit card #1. You will continue to do this until this credit card is completely paid off. Once you've achieved this, any extra money at the end of the month will go towards mom and dad's personal loan until it's completely paid off, so on and so on.

The AVALANCHE METHOD – Compound interest is what credit card and loan companies are charging you on a monthly basis. In some cases, this can be as high as 29% annually. Compound interest is what makes credit card companies rich and keeps you broke.
Compound interest is also what will make you rich, which you will see further into this program. It's now time to list all your credit cards and loans from the highest interest rate to the lowest interest rate. As you did in the snowball method, you will take the excess money from your monthly budget and apply it to the largest interest rate balance first. You will continue to do this each month, until this debt is paid off. Note, the debt with the highest interest rate could possibly be the debt with the highest balance, and therefore take a longer time to pay off. Once the highest interest rate debt is paid off, then you will move on to the next highest interest rate, so on and so on, until all your debt balances are gone.

The purpose of paying debt off by using the avalanche method is strictly math. By paying off the highest interest rate first, you're getting rid of those nasty interest charges that you're paying to make other people wealthy.

An example of the avalanche method repayment schedule would be as shown below.

Credit card #1　　　　　$150 balance after minimum payment 25% interest

Car loan　　　　　　　$5,000 balance after minimum payment 9% interest

Student loan　　　　　$19,500 balance after minimum payment 6% interest

Loan to mom & dad　　$1,000 balance 0% interest

After all minimum payments have been made, any extra money will be applied to credit card #1. With a nasty interest rate of 25%, you can't get rid of this debt fast enough. Do whatever you can to get this paid off permanently.

Once you've achieved this, any extra money at the end of the month will go towards the car loan, with an interest rate of 9%. You will continue the extra payments on this until it's completely paid off, so on and so on.

SAVING & INVESTING

Congratulations, you've gotten yourself out of debt, and grinded through the painstaking part of your journey. For the past months, several months, or even years, you've watched your debt balances decline to the point that they've completely disappeared. What you just accomplished is amazing. Make sure you take the time to realize what you've accomplished. Now you're ready for the fun part of personal finance. You are about to witness the miracle of compound interest work in your favor. Every dollar you save and/or invest, compound interest is working for you and not against you. This will make your net worth grow faster than you ever thought possible. Let's discuss the difference between savings and investing, and why we need to do both.

Saving (Emergency Fund) In the journey of personal finance, savings should be looked at in a couple of ways. First, everyone should have enough saved to have an emergency fund of 3 – 6 months of expenses. Your emergency fund is the savings account that your parents or grandparents told you to "save for a rainy day". Trust me, it's going to rain.

Be prepared for that rainy day with your emergency fund of 3-6 months of expenses. 70% of Americans can't sustain an emergency of $1,000 without putting it on their credit card. You just got done paying off your credit cards, don't fall back into that trap again. Cars break down, water heaters break, roofs need to be replaced, medical expenses arise, jobs are not guaranteed. By having an emergency fund of 3-6 months of expenses, this allows you a cushion. If (when) your emergency appears, you'll be prepared. At least more prepared than not having any emergency fund at all.

If your monthly household expenses are $4,000 per month, your emergency fund should be $12,000 to $24,000. This money is NOT to be invested anywhere. This needs to be looked at as insurance and should be in a place where you can have quick access to it. A local bank or credit union are perfect places for your emergency fund. Unfortunately, banks and credit unions are typically paying less than 1% interest, so you're not going to get rich on your emergency fund. Another place to park your emergency fund would be an online bank paying a high yield interest rate of 4% - 5% currently. Online institutions can afford to pay a little higher interest rates because they don't have the expense of a brick-and-mortar facility. Do your due diligence and research your potential online institution prior to depositing your emergency fund.

Many of these institutions will be FDIC insured, but please verify that ahead of time. Also keep in mind that if (when) you will need to access your emergency fund because your rainy day has arrived, it may take up to three days to have your funds transferred from your online bank to your local institution. Having a fully funded emergency fund in place, turns that emergency into an inconvenience.

Savings (Sinking Funds) A sinking fund is a separate savings account (or this can be an envelope) for something that you know is coming up and you want to be prepared for. This could be a new car purchase, a vacation, a new home, a home repair or remodel, Christmas or birthday gifts, etc. A sinking fund can be one larger pot of money that any of these listed items can be taken from, or they can be categorized accounts or envelopes for each item. That's up to you. Sinking funds are usually expenditures that you'd expect to come up within the next 12 months or so. Again, this should not be looked at as an investment.

Investing – There are several types of investing options available. Which option you choose is up to you. You can start a business or invest in an existing business. You can invest in various forms of real estate. The most common form of investing is in the stock market. This can be through an employer 401K plan, a personal IRA or a personal brokerage account. This is the form we're going to concentrate on next.

When we talk about investing, we're always referring to LONG TERM investing. Investing is designed to be for your future stability, not an effort to get some quick cash to make ends meet by the end of the month. We're talking years and even decades. Before deciding which path is best for you, you must get to know yourself. By that, I mean, how tolerant are you when it comes to the ups and downs of the stock market on any given day? If the market trends upwards for two weeks straight, are you looking to cash out by selling your shares and run off with the quick profits? Or when the market trends downwards for two weeks straight, are you looking for the nearest ledge to jump from, cash out before you "lose all your money"? If your personality fits either of these two scenarios, then maybe stock market investing isn't for you. The one guarantee of the stock market is that it will be volatile. Let's move forward and discuss some of the basic ways to invest in the stock market.

401K – (403B or TSP) is a retirement account that is set up by your employer for your benefit. This has taken the place of the former pension plans that were often offered by various employers. Currently, pension plans have mostly been continued by unions and government entities. By the government allowing the benefit of a 401K plan, this allows the individual to be more responsible for their own future retirement. As of 2024, the maximum allowable annual contribution for an individual to contribute to their 401K retirement plan is $23,000 ($30,500 if you're over the age of 50). Not in all cases, but in many cases, the employer will match a certain percentage of your contribution to YOUR 401K plan. This percentage amount will vary with each employer, but it's fairly common to see a 1% - 5% match from your employer. Here's a table of what that might look like.

Employee Salary		$50,000
Employee 401K Contribution	5%	$2,500
Employer Match	5%	$2,500

      This is $2,500 of free money from your employer!! Why would you NOT take advantage of this? There is a "vesting" schedule that most employers will put in place to entice their employees to stay with the company for a longer length of time. Here's how the vesting schedule works. Anything that you ever contribute to your 401K retirement account is yours to keep. Nobody can take that away from you. However, the amount of money contributed to your 401K retirement account via your employer's match, is very often attached to a vesting schedule. The vesting schedule is typically set up whereas the longer you stay, the more of the employer's match you get to keep. The sooner you leave, the more money you may be forfeiting from the employer's match. Here's a typical vesting schedule.

Length of Employment	Percentage you keep of employer's match
After 1 year of employment	20%
After 2 years of employment	40%
After 3 years of employment	60%
After 4 years of employment	80%
After 5 years of employment	100%

401K Traditional vs Roth – Now that you know basically how a 401K works, let's learn the difference between a traditional and Roth account. A traditional 401K account is considered a "pretax" retirement account. This means that from your weekly paycheck, the amount of your 401K contribution is the first item deducted from your gross amount. This money is not taxed by the federal or state government at this time. This is also known as a tax advantaged account, as you are essentially receiving a tax deduction in the year of your contribution. Once your contribution is deducted from your gross amount, then the balance of your paycheck will be taxed accordingly.

See the chart below

Gross Pay	$1,000
401K Contribution	$100
Taxable Paycheck Amount	$900
Federal Tax	
State Tax	
FICA	

    When you reach the age of 59 ½ years of age, you will then be allowed to withdraw from your retirement account without any penalties. Any money that is withdrawn after the age of 59 ½ will be susceptible to federal and state income taxes at the time of withdrawal and will be treated as regular income. If you withdraw any amount from your retirement account before the age of 59 ½ years of age, you will be assessed a 10% penalty for early withdrawal. Withdrawing money from your retirement account is highly discouraged in the personal finance community, except in the most extreme situations.

    If you were to invest $100 per week in your 401K retirement account between the ages of 25 through 60 and earn an average of 10% interest per year, you can expect to have approximately $1,850,000 at the end of 35 years. You would have contributed $182,000 during that time frame ($100 per week x 52 weeks x 35 years = $182,000) and $1,668,000 is the result of compounding interest over 35 years. Albert Einstein coined the phrase "compound interest is the 8th wonder of the world". You can see why. Keep in mind that 100% of the money withdrawn from your account after the age of 59 ½ years of age is susceptible to federal and state income tax.

Roth 401K – This is considered an after-tax retirement account. Whereas in the traditional 401K account, your contribution was taken from your paycheck prior to federal and state taxes being withheld, with the Roth account your federal and state taxes are being withheld on all of your earnings, before you contribute to your Roth account. At this point you may be wondering, why on earth would I want to do that? Patience, and you will see the massive advantages of the Roth.

Because this is still considered a retirement account, the same access limitations are placed on this account. The money will not be available for withdrawal until the age of 59 ½ years of age. 10% penalties are accessed upon withdrawal if done so prior to the age 59 ½. There are some exceptions to this rule, but to cover the basics, we won't get involved in these weeds.

So, you've made it to the age of 60 and you've been contributing $100 per week for the past 35 years at an average of 10% interest per year, just as you have in the Traditional 401K chart above. You've accumulated approximately the same amount of $1,850,000. You've contributed the same $182,000 over that time frame and realized the same growth of $1,668,000. Can you hear the drum roll? Upon withdrawal of your money after the age of 59 ½ years of age, with the Roth 401K you will pay $0 in federal and state income taxes. You were already taxed on the $182,000 of contributions before you invested in your Roth, and your account was allowed to grow tax free forever.

In either scenario, the traditional or Roth, compound interest is working for you. When you're in debt, the interest payments that you're making have the same compound interest at work, but it's working against you. Which would you prefer?

IRA – Individual Retirement Accounts work similar to the 401K accounts. There is a traditional version and a Roth version. These would be accounts that you would set up on your own, and not through your employer. Therefore, there is no possibility of a match situation. Whatever you contribute, is what you get. The traditional account will be tax advantaged (pretax) and the Roth account will be after tax, similar to the 401K accounts. The biggest difference between the IRA accounts and the 401K accounts is the maximum allowable contributions per year. As of 2024, the maximum allowable contribution for the IRA is $7,000 ($8,000 over the age of 50) per year. All other facets of the accounts are similar.

When the time comes for you to leave your employer for another employer or even retirement, one thing you don't want to do is leave your 401K retirement account behind. You also don't want your old 401K company writing you a check for the full amount. If not handled properly, the IRS may look at this as a withdrawal from your account and assessing you with a 10% penalty on the entire amount. You have a couple options at this point. Your new employer may allow you to roll over a previous 401K retirement account into their 401K retirement account. This is an entirely acceptable thing to do. Provide your new 401K company with all the account information of your previous 401K company, and they will facilitate the transaction for you. You may have to sign a form or two, but this is the cleanest way of moving your retirement account safely. You want the funds from your previous 401K to transfer directly to your new 401K without you touching the money at all.

If your new 401K company does not allow you to roll over a previous 401K, then you can simply have your IRA company contact your previous 401K company and have them facilitate the roll over transaction. Again, you don't want these funds delivered directly to you. At the point of rolling over old 401K accounts into new 401K accounts or IRA accounts, it is imperative that any traditional accounts are rolled over into traditional accounts, and any Roth accounts are rolled over into Roth accounts. Any cross over of types of accounts can result in IRS penalties.

Brokerage Accounts – Are considered to be after tax accounts. Stock market investing, in its simplest forms, can be done in three ways. By purchasing individual stocks for one or more companies, by purchasing mutual funds, or by purchasing index funds. A nice thing about having a brokerage account is that there are no maximum limits as to how much you can invest.

When you purchase an individual stock, you're purchasing a share or several shares in a particular company. You are then actually becoming the owner of that company. That's right, if you purchase one share of Apple stock, then you own a very small percentage of that company. Your balance will increase as the overall stock price of this company rises, and your balance will decrease as the overall stock price of this company falls. If that company offers a quarterly dividend, you will receive that in your account with the option of cashing that out or reinvesting it back into your account.

    Purchasing individual stocks is considered one of the riskier ways of investing in the stock market. It can have higher rewards, because as this company grows, your profits grow. At the same time, the company may struggle and lose value, as will your account. Your investment in this one stock purchase is solely reliable on this one company's ability to perform for you. It is possible for this one company's value to double, triple, quadruple or even more. The same possibility exists for that company's value to decrease by 50%, 75% or even go out of business completely, leaving you with a $0 balance. This is considered high volatility.

When you purchase a mutual fund, you're purchasing a share or several shares in one mutual fund. That one mutual fund will include 100's or even 1,000's of individual companies. That's right, for the same price you may invest in one individual stock, you can own one mutual fund share and own a very small piece of many different companies. The benefit in owning a mutual fund, is when you own several different companies, one of those companies may struggle and even go out of business. However, the many other companies within that mutual fund may do well and offset the losses you may have otherwise encountered. With a mutual fund, in a good year you may see a 20% profit. In a bad year, you may see a 20% decline. Most years will be somewhere in between.

The volatility is not nearly as high as purchasing individual stocks, and therefore considered to be a much more stable way to invest. One thing to keep in mind is that a mutual fund comes with a mutual fund manager. This is not a person you will ever meet, but he/she is the person responsible for managing this fund. This will include deciding which companies to include within this mutual fund and which companies to eliminate from this mutual fund. This is monitored on a regular basis by the fund manager. The fund manager charges a very small nominal fee to the mutual fund shareholders. This percentage can typically run between .5% - 3%. Many feel this is a very small price to pay for allowing the manager to work on the details behind the scenes.

This brings us to the third way of getting into the stock market, and that would be by purchasing index funds. Index funds work in the same manner as mutual funds, as they include 100's and 1,000's of individual companies within their funds. Index funds are funds that mimic some of the Wall Street indexes, such as the S&P500. Index funds are systematically calibrated to add the better performing companies and eliminate the poorer performing companies. This is done automatically and does not have a manager who is actively managing the funds. For this reason, the percentage charges can typically run between 0% - .5%. Some feel that the lower fees charged are worth going with index funds over mutual funds. Some feel that the managed funds are more likely to realize better profitability than index funds, and therefore choose the mutual funds.

The type of account, 401K, IRA, traditional, Roth, Brokerage all depends on what your long-term goals are. This will definitely vary from one person to another. There's no wrong answer here, it's whatever you want out of life. If retiring early at the age of 40, 45 or 50 is your goal, that's great. Investing in a brokerage account is probably the best option for you. After all, investing all your funds in a retirement account, where you can't access the funds until you're 59 ½ years old, doesn't really seem to meet the needs of your long-term goal of retiring early. On the other hand, if you plan to work until full retirement age, then a 401K retirement plan may be more suited for you. If your employer doesn't provide a 401K retirement plan, then there's always the IRA. You'll have to determine whether the traditional or Roth is best for you.

Day Trading – THIS IS NOT INVESTING. Day trading is the act of buying individual stocks, holding them for hours or days, and trying to "time the market" just right and sell for a quick profit. This is not considered investing, but rather speculating. Your "system" is not fool proof. In the long run, you run the very likely risk of losing more times than you win, losing more money than you won, or even worse, losing all of what you originally started with. This is no more investing than going to Vegas and playing the slot machines, going to the convenience store for those scratch tickets, or betting on the winner in tonight's big game. Don't be fooled by the dopamine rush you'll get from that first quick trade that made you a quick $100. The IRS considers this a short-term gain as opposed to a long-term gain (as you would find in investments held for more than one year) and therefore will tax you at your regular income tax rate instead of the 15% capitol gains rate of a long-term gain.

REAL ESTATE

Real estate investing is a topic which can revolve around many different forms of investing. Here again, we will try and cover the basics. There will always be additional information available through various internet searches, books and podcasts.

First, know what is and what isn't considered an investment, when it comes to real estate. Renting any form of real estate, whether it be an apartment, a condominium or a single-family home, is not considered investing. It may fulfill a need for obtaining shelter for yourself and your family, but it simply is not considered investing. Purchasing a condo or a single family as your primary residence is typically not considered an investment. It is true that this type of property can and most likely will increase in value over time but is not considered investing. It is also true that it is possible to profit from this type of property but is still not considered investing.

Primary Residence – So you've purchased a single-family home or condominium as your primary residence. You have a spare room, basement or garage that's doing nothing but collecting dust and becoming a "catch all" for all your must have purchases that you are no longer using. The term "House Hacking" has been coined by Scott Trench from the Bigger Pockets Money podcast. It's a very simple idea that people have been doing for years before it was ever given a name. Rent out that spare bedroom, basement or garage to a trustworthy person in exchange for payment. This extra payment can go towards paying down your outstanding debts, paying down your mortgage, building up your emergency account, contributing towards your sinking funds, contributing towards your IRA retirement account, contributing towards your brokerage account. The possibilities are endless.

If your primary home is a condominium, you may have to check with your HOA to see if there are any restrictions against having a tenant living in your property. Also, when renting out any space to someone, you want to be extremely careful in vetting your prospective tenant. In a house hacking situation, the tenant will typically have access to the common areas of the property, and therefore be "all up in your business". You want to make sure that you are very compatible with your live in tenant.

Multi Family Property or Secondary Single-Family Home – Whether this property is a single-family home separate from your primary residence, a two family, three family or four family, they are all considered investment properties. Obviously, you can purchase a five-unit property or larger, but depending on your community, this may be considered a commercial property and therefore have different rules and regulations. We are going to stick with the smaller residential properties.

By owning this type of property, it is most likely that your main objective is to make money and grow your wealth. If this is the case, then you need to be sure that prior to purchasing your property, research other properties in the area. See what the recent sales prices have been, and if possible, learn what can be expected to receive in the form of rent payments from your tenants. You want to be sure that the rent income you receive monthly is more than your expenses for the property. This would include all your expenses, such as mortgage payments, insurance, taxes any utilities, trash removal, lawn care, snow removal, property maintenance, etc. In making these calculations, you also want to assume that your property will NOT be rented for 12 months out of the year. There is always a period between one tenant leaving and the next tenant moving in, where the unit will be unoccupied. This loss of income needs to be figured as an expense to the property.

Once you have your property up and running and fully rented, you are officially a landlord. The better landlord you are to your tenants, the more likely you'll attract better tenants. Make sure to keep complete and accurate financial records of all income received and expenses paid throughout the year. You are theoretically running a business and when filing your annual taxes, your accountant will take full advantage of the tax laws in your favor.

FIND YOUR PURPOSE

You've discovered this by accident, it was given to you by someone who cares, or you blindly came across it while searching for something else. Regardless of how you found it, you found it. Now what are you going to do with the information you've just learned about? Are you currently in debt, sick and tired of being sick and tired? Have you had enough? Do you work too hard to be this broke? These are all common phrases that we've all used in the world of personal finance.

Or maybe you're out of debt and figured you're doing just fine now. As you've just discovered, you can always be doing a whole lot better.

Maybe retiring early has a certain ring to it. Maybe having more money can provide you with more pleasurable options later in life, like scaling back work hours, spending more time with family and friends, or spoiling yourself later in life when you can afford it.

Find your purpose. Apply what you've learned to your lifestyle. What I've spelled out for you is easily repeatable. Trust me, if I can do it, anyone can. I challenge you to take that first step. If you don't like the progress you make after a period, it's your life, you can always go back in debt. The more entrenched you become with paying attention to your finances, the more research you'll do on your own to accelerate your wealth growth.

    My purpose in writing this is to inspire others to succeed with money as I have, and many others. In too many households, for too many years, it's been tabooed to speak openly about personal finances. My parents never talked about finances to me or my siblings. Their parents never talked to them about finances, just as so many families never talked about finances. One of the main reasons for this is that personal finance has mostly never been taught in our education systems. If you're never taught about something, how will you ever learn. There is a personal finance movement out there today, and the acronym is FIRE. Finance Independence Retire Early. If this book lights a fire within you, I urge you to search for more information on this topic.

PERSONAL TESTIMONIAL

I was born and raised into a middle-income family. My father was the provider for the family. He was a self-employed drywall contractor and worked endlessly. My mom was a stay-at-home mom. She cooked, cleaned, sewed and was able to stretch a dollar as far as it could possibly go. My three siblings and I never wanted for anything, but we were the furthest thing from spoiled children as could be. We weren't given many "extras" and we all learned early on, that if you wanted something, you'd have to work for it.

In 1986, at the age of 22, I got married and bought my first house. We had the world by the balls, or so we thought. We had our first child 2 years later. Within the next year, I quit my job and started a window construction company with a friend of mine. We had both worked in the industry for about 5 years by then and thought we knew it all. We seemed to make mistake after mistake, always thinking we were doing the right thing. We borrowed money from family. The economy turned bad and finding the next project was always a battle. We then had our second child. We struggled incredibly for the next few years, living off of credit cards, never being able to pay off all the bills in any given month, running out of heating oil on more than one occasion in those cold New England winters, and discovering macaroni & cheese as a pantry staple.

After about 5 years, we dissolved the window company and after a year of searching, I finally found a company that would hire me. Always staying within the window industry, I bounced around from one company to another, year after year. At the same time, I took the skills that I learned from being self employed and created a side hustle of installing windows in the evenings and weekends. I had made a promise to myself that if I ever got our family out of the financial debt from the previous 5 years, that I would never put us in that position again. It took a few years to clear up the debt, move out of our starter home and into a nicer, safer neighborhood. A couple more years on this projection, and we upscaled in home and neighborhood once again.

All is going great, or so I thought. I had discovered the internet and online stock trading. Purchased a stock that had been doing well. It kept splitting, doubling our money again and again, and just like that, the company went out of business, and we just lost $35,000. It wasn't long after that that my wife and I divorced. Sold the house, divided the assets, and started over. I remarried within two years and three years later, divorced again. This time I kept the house, but still had to divide the assets and start over. Just when things were steam rolling ahead, I got divorced twice and just saw no possible way to ever get ahead again. Life had me by the balls by this time.

With my growing knowledge of the industry I'd given my life to, both as my primary source of income and my side hustle, things were about to take off. I changed employers for one last time. This, along with the side hustle for a couple more years, catapulted me to places I'd never been before financially. From here I saw the income I was achieving and decided I needed to educate myself on how to handle this newly found wealth. Listening to financial podcasts, reading blogs and financial books became my new side hustle. Soaking it all in and learning what I should do next. I had previously contributed an obligatory 5%-10% to my 401K, but with the information I was absorbing, I began maxing out my retirement contributions. A lifelong dream of mine was to live in Florida. I purchased a single-family home and became a long-distance landlord, with the help of my nephew. A year later, I approached my employer to allow me to work remotely from Florida, as it was time to live my dream. Much to my surprise, he agreed. I purchased yet another house to use as my primary residence. This was my third property. My original house in Rhode Island was now a rental, my first Florida home was a second rental and my new primary home. With no consumer debt at all, except for my three mortgages, it was time to get to work and eliminate ALL of my debt. Within 5 years, I had all three mortgages paid off. I cannot stress enough how important it is to be on the same page with your spouse while on this journey. Due to family health issues, my now wife (who was by my side and encouraged me every day for the past 15 years) and I moved back to Rhode Island to be closer with the family. We started selling off the houses one by one and putting the proceeds into after tax brokerage accounts.

At this point, I'm looking at early retirement in the not-too-distant future, a very healthy portfolio that consists of two properties (one primary home and one rental), well above average retirement accounts and a brokerage account that I plan to live off in my retirement years. Filing for social security isn't a thought or necessity.

I felt that giving my own testimonial with money will serve you well in a few different ways. One, you don't have to be perfect to win with money. I've made more than my fair share of mistakes with money. Two, you don't need to start at the age of 18-20 to win with money. We all wish we can go back in time and start investing at an earlier age, but the truth is, it's never too late to start. Three, take some risks, allow yourself to make mistakes, and learn from those mistakes. Don't be afraid to flex your risk muscle. Four, you're never too old to begin your successful journey with money. I never went to college and didn't have the traditional formal education. What I did have was the work ethic given to me by my father. I never ever saw him quit on anything, and I never gave up either. My mother taught me to be frugal. I watched her stretch those family dollars, and I take great pride in knowing how to do the same. I learned how to make money work for me and implemented what I learned. I discovered the beauty of having compound interest work for me!!

www.ingramcontent.com/pod-product-compliance
Lightning Source LLC
Chambersburg PA
CBHW072054230526
45479CB00010B/1064